Majbritt Greve
Michael Wendelboe Hansen
Henrik Schaumburg-Müller

CONTAINER SHIPPING AND ECONOMIC DEVELOPMENT

A Case Study of A.P. Moller - Maersk in South East Asia

Copenhagen Business School Press

Container Shipping and Economic Development
A Case Study of A.P. Moller - Maersk in South East Asia

Printed in Denmark by Narayana Press, Gylling
Book design, typeset and cover design by BUSTO | Graphic Design
Cover image: A.P. Moller - Maersk

1st edition 2007

ISBN 13: 978-87-630-0213-4

Distribution:

Scandinavia
DJOEF/DBK, Mimersvej 4
DK-4600 Køge, Denmark
Tel +45 3269 7788, fax +45 3269 7789

North America
International Specialized Book Services
920 NE 58th Ave., Suite 300
Portland, OR 97213, USA
Tel +1 800 944 6190, fax +1 503 280 8832
Email: orders@isbs.com

Rest of the World
Marston Book Services, P.O. Box 269
Abingdon, Oxfordshire, OX14 4YN, UK
Tel +44 (0) 1235 465500, fax +44 (0) 1235 4656555
E-mail Direct Customers: direct.order@marston.co.uk
E-mail Booksellers: trade.order@marston.co.uk

CONTAINER SHIPPING AND ECONOMIC DEVELOPMENT

A Case Study of A.P. Moller - Maersk in South East Asia

Table of Contents

Preface

The academic literature is surprisingly weak when it comes to conceptualising and analysing the role of transport in economic development. Although the Development Economics literature acknowledges that transport plays a role as a facilitator of trade and economic development, this role is theoretically underdeveloped and empirically under-explored. In addition, while the International Business literature has investigated so-called 'spillover' effects of foreign direct investment by multinational corporations (MNCs) in general, little has been said about spillover effects from foreign direct investment by transport MNCs specifically. In order to fill some of the lacunas in the received literature, a team of researchers from Copenhagen Business School's Centre for Business and Development Studies decided to undertake an explorative case study of the world's largest container shipping firm, A.P. Moller - Maersk, and its role in integrating developing countries and their firms into the global economy. The study focused on A.P. Moller - Maersk's container business in South East Asian developing countries, and in particular Vietnam. This book presents the main findings of the study.

We wish to express our sincere gratitude to A.P. Moller - Maersk in Singapore and Vietnam for giving us the opportunity to study this important Danish company from a novel perspective. We would also like to thank the Danish Research Council for Development Research and the Centre for Business and Development Studies for financial assistance to the project.

Majbritt Greve
Michael Wendelboe Hansen
Henrik Schaumburg-Müller

Copenhagen
June 2007

CHAPTER 1

Background to the Study

From the regional headquarters of A.P. Moller - Maersk in South East Asia, which overlooks the port of Singapore, the dynamic growth of global seaborne trade and the increasing synchronisation of global trade are readily apparent. Ever larger container ships are lined up at the harbour's entrance, containers are stacked as far as the eye can see and Panamax cranes are working day and night to reduce the ships' turn-around time in the port. This is an image of the global economy where production processes are dispersed across ever-larger geographical distance, and where the coordination of multiple modes of transport, vast flows of information, and inter-organisational relationships are increasingly vital.

Source: Majbritt Greve

A.P. Moller - Maersk is by far Denmark's largest firm with an annual net turnover of more than 44 billion USD,[1] of which the container business and related activities account for more than 25 billion USD.[2]

---

[1] A.P. Moller - Maersk's total market capitalisation value in 2006 amounted to almost 38 billion USD (Annual Report for 2006 for A.P. Møller – Mærsk A/S, www.maersk.com).
[2] Annual Report for 2006 for A.P. Møller – Mærsk A/S (www.maersk.com).

It is also one of the largest Danish foreign investors – in 2005[3] alone A.P. Moller - Maersk invested more than 10 billion USD globally, mainly in ships, port terminals, oil activities and IT.[4] Maersk Line is the world's largest container shipping firm accounting for approximately 15-20% of global container shipping transport. It transports goods worth billions of dollars annually from the factory floors of South East Asia to the shops of New York, London, Paris and other commercial centres around the world. Ultimately, Maersk is making it possible for producers in the South to reach consumers in the North, thus potentially having a major impact on economic development.

Yet, in spite of the almost global reach of A.P. Moller - Maersk and its huge potential impact on developing countries, no one to our knowledge has studied the role of A.P. Moller - Maersk in integrating developing countries into the global economy. Thus, the goal of this study is to understand the role of A.P. Moller - Maersk's container business in integrating developing countries and their firms into the global economy. This is done by analysing A.P. Moller - Maersk's container business activities in South East Asia with particular emphasis on A.P. Moller - Maersk's activities in Vietnam.

The Literature on Transport and Economic Development

The theoretical and empirical literature on the role of transport in economic development is surprisingly weak. In general, transport is acknowledged to play an important role as a facilitator of economic development; however, the role of transport remains ambiguous and subject to shallow interpretations (Pedersen, 2001; Goetz and Rodrigue, 1999; Janelle and Beuthe, 1997; Leinbach, 1995).

While development and trade economists originally considered the cost of transport in economic development (Pedersen, 2002), the role of transport largely disappeared from mainstream trade and development economics in the 1970s, possibly due to falling transport costs as a consequence of advances in transport and communication technology. More recently, some trade and development economists have 'rediscovered' the role of transport in economic

[3] Accordingly, the A.P. Moller - Maersk Group invested more than 5.5 billion dollars in 2006 (Annual Report for 2006 for A.P. Møller – Mærsk, www.maersk.com).

[4] Annual Report for 2005 for A.P. Møller – Mærsk A/S (www.maersk.com).

development (e.g.: Krugman, 1997 and Janelle and Beuthe, 1997), however these accounts generally fail to recognize transport as an integral and holistic aspect of production and distribution systems (Pedersen, 2001).

Within the International Business literature, there is a long-standing tradition for investigating so-called 'spillover effects' (positive externalities) from foreign direct investment (for reviews of this literature, see Blomstrøm & Kokko, 2000 or Meyer, 2003). However, this literature generally fails to embrace the developmental role of the service sector in general and of the shipping and logistics industry in particular.

Within the Global Value Chain literature, the integration of developing countries into global value chains (GVCs) has been studied extensively (e.g.: Gereffi et al., 2001; Gereffi, 1994; Gereffi et al., 1994). This literature examines the governance structures in global value chains, partly in order to explain the international division of labour. Here, lead firms in core countries are seen as initiating, coordinating and governing global value chains, and hence specifying what is to be produced by whom and in which locations. A key concern for this literature is to understand how developing country firms can link up to GVCs and gain access to higher value–added activities in the chain. Thus, the GVC literature explicitly addresses the integration of developing country producers into the global economy. However, here we also find a missing link in regard to transport services, even though, as expressed by Rabach and Kim,

> *services have come to play a critical role in GCCs (Global Commodity Chains), because they not only provide geographical and transactional connections, but they integrate and coordinate the atomised and globalised production processes. Without the integrating and coordinating functions fulfilled by services, GCCs would not be viable in today's highly competitive economic environment* (Rabach and Kim, 1994:123).

Thus, our overall impression is that there exists a lacuna in the literature in regard to the role of transport and logistics firms in economic development. Nevertheless, there are literatures where we can find inspiration for a study of the role of shipping in integrating developing countries into the global economy.

In this study, we are inspired first by the value chain approach as developed by Porter (1985), and more specifically the modifications of Porter's value chain approach by Fjeldstad and Stabell (1998). Fjeldstad and Stabell identify three distinct value configuration modes, namely 'value chains', 'value shops' and 'value networks'. Basically, the value chain (long-linked technology) delivers value by transforming inputs into products; the value shop (intensive technology) by resolving unique customer problems; and the value network (mediating technology) by enabling direct and indirect exchanges between customers. Fjeldstad and Stabell characterize the transport sector as a value network that creates value by enabling direct and indirect exchanges between customers, or in other words by performing an intermediary role in value chains.

Secondly, we try to understand the intermediary role of shipping in more detail with inspiration from the supply chain management literature, and in particular the notions of 'third' (3PL) and 'fourth' party logistics (4PL) providers (Berglund et al., 1999; Lieb, 2005).[5] The notions of 3PL and 4PL refer to the activities that a logistics provider carries out on behalf of a shipper. The activities include a wide range of services from management and execution of transport and warehousing to value added services such as supply chain management and even secondary assembly (Berglund et al., 1999:59).

Methodology

The unit of analysis of this study is A.P. Moller - Maersk's container business in South East Asia with particular emphasis on their operations in Vietnam. Although the company over time has diversified into other major business areas including energy, offshore activities, manufacturing and air-transport, container shipping remains A.P. Moller - Maersk's core business.

South East Asia is well suited for a case study of A.P. Moller - Maersk's role in integrating developing countries into the global economy. In particular, South East Asia is the third fastest growing economic area in the world measured in terms of GDP growth, and the region is home to a number of

[5] According to Schary et al., (2001:228-230), the concept of 4PL captures the highest degree of cooperation between the client and the logistics operator. It involves the provision of a broad range of services of strategic importance. It involves the outsourcing of management and logistics services, from traditional services such as warehousing, transportation and other value added services to managing and optimising the supply chain by focusing on information technology and global coverage. The provider may take the role of a so-called lead logistics provider responsible for securing a complete package of services. 4PL relationships are long-term arrangements in which firms are organisationally highly integrated and asset specificity is high. In other words, the logistics operator may invest in client dedicated facilities, specialised handling equipment, exchange of personnel and specialised training programmes.

emerging and developing countries that outperform other emerging regions in terms of export oriented manufacturing. Moreover, South East Asia hosts four of the world's largest ports that together account for 13% of global container traffic (ISL, 2005:11-12).

A.P. Moller - Maersk in Vietnam is interesting due to Vietnam's huge potential for economic development and A.P. Moller - Maersk's strong market position and long history of operating in Vietnam. In particular, Maersk Vietnam Ltd. was one of the first foreign, container-shipping operators to be granted a license to operate as a 100% foreign owned entity. For all of these reasons, a study of A.P. Moller - Maersk in Vietnam is well suited to illustrate some of the possible developmental implications of container shipping for developing economies that are rapidly and massively moving towards an export orientation.

This study is the product of intensive data collection and participant observation of A.P. Moller - Maersk and external partners conducted in Singapore in 2006 and in Vietnam in 2003 and 2006. In 2006, almost 30 interviews were conducted and extensive documentation was collected from various units of the A.P. Moller - Maersk Group (Maersk Line, Maersk Logistics, APM Terminals, MCC transport) and some of their main customers in Singapore and Vietnam. In 2003, more than 30 interviews were conducted and supporting material was collected from A.P. Moller - Maersk, their customers, their subcontractors, agents, their joint venture partners, and several international organisations.

Outline of the Book

The book has four chapters. After the Introduction, Chapter 2 provides an overview of the organisation, activities and strategies of A.P. Moller - Maersk's container business. The chapter emphasises both A.P. Moller - Maersk's global strategy and the company's specific strategy for South East Asia. The purpose of the chapter is partly to introduce the company and partly to lay the ground for the subsequent analysis of the role of A.P. Moller - Maersk's container business in integrating developing countries into global value chains. Chapter 3, which is the core of the book, will assess A.P. Moller - Maersk's role in integrating developing countries into the global economy. This analysis is divided into two major areas:

- A.P. Moller - Maersk's role in building physical container-transport infrastructure

- A.P. Moller - Maersk's role in integrating and coordinating globalised production processes.

Thus, the chapter explores the effects that A.P. Moller - Maersk's container business may have in terms of integrating developing countries into global value chains and the factors that explain these effects. Essentially, the effects of A.P. Moller - Maersk's activities will be viewed partly as a function of the company's strategies, and partly as a function of host country characteristics (in particular Vietnam's) such as infrastructure, legislation and absorptive capacity of local industry.[6] Finally, Chapter 4 sums up the conclusions of the study.

[6] Several authors analyze the effects of FDI in terms of investor strategy and host country endowments. For example, see Narula et al. (2003), Lauridsen (2003), Altenburg (2000), Dicken (1998) and Dunning (1997).

CHAPTER 2

Introducing A.P. Moller - Maersk's Container Business

Before we move on to an analysis of the role of A.P. Moller - Maersk's container business in global value chain integration, we will characterize the business and the strategies underlying it. In particular, we provide a description of the organisation, activities and strategies of the core of A.P. Moller - Maersk's container business.

The Corporate Structure of A.P. Moller – Maersk

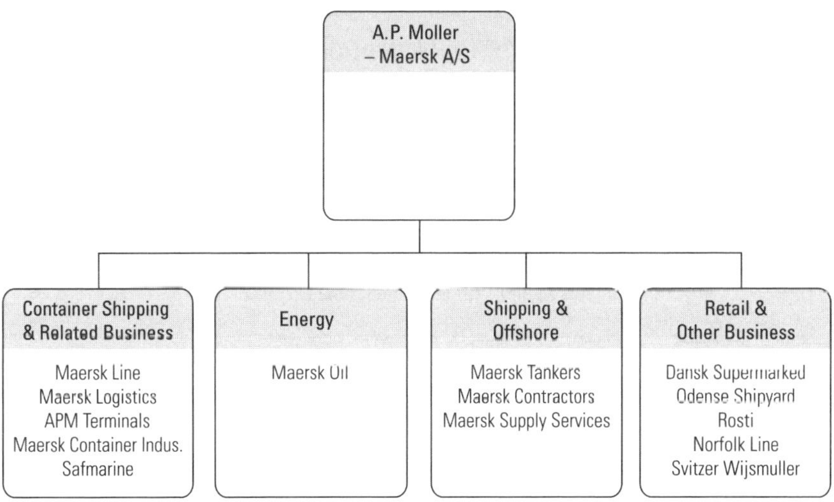

Source: Authors, as inspired by www.maersk.com

The Overall Structure of A.P. Moller - Maersk's Container Business

From a modest beginning in steam shipping in 1904, A.P. Moller - Maersk has grown into a global conglomerate diversified across business areas such as energy, shipping and offshore, retail and other businesses (refer to figure above). Container shipping, however, remains the traditional core activity of A.P. Moller - Maersk. A.P. Moller - Maersk's container business includes several independent business units such as Maersk Line, Maersk Logistics, APM Terminals, Maersk Container Industry and Safmarine. For illustrative purposes, the container business of A.P. Moller - Maersk can be characterized as consisting of essentially three pillars: Maersk Line/Safmarine, APM Terminals and Maersk Logistics. Maersk Line and Safmarine provide global container-liner services with Maersk Line being the most prominent firm. Safmarine is the result of an acquisition of the South African container line of the same name. The two other pillars, APM Terminals and Maersk Logistics, are the result of A.P. Moller - Maersk's expansive growth and diversification strategy. APM Terminals builds and operates container terminals, while Maersk Logistics provides integrated logistics services. Both of these operations are conducted on a global scale. A.P. Moller - Maersk has also diversified into providing other container related services, such as Maersk container industry, which is involved in designing, producing and marketing containers. For simplicity however, the following analysis will focus on what we consider to be the three main pillars of A.P. Moller - Maersk's container activities: Maersk Line, Maersk Logistics and APM Terminals.

The Three Pillars of A.P. Moller – Maersk's Container Business

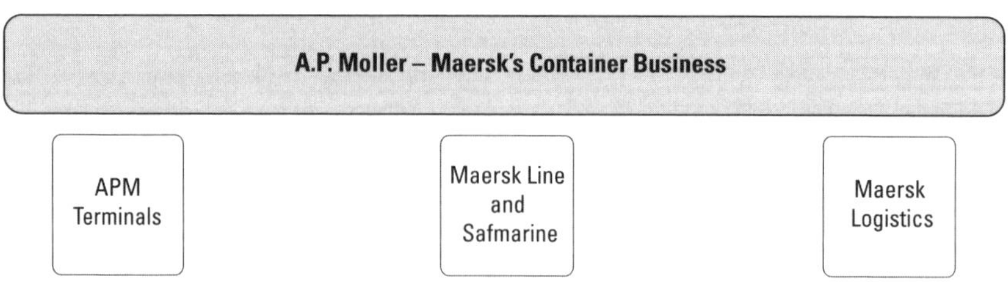

Source: Authors

Each of these units operates as an independent firm that interacts with the others on market terms and is evaluated as a separate profit and loss centre. In particular, each unit may offer its services to competing operators. Operating these entities as individual units allows A.P. Moller - Maersk to be more cost oriented. The units, however, are also complementary and able to create synergies by cooperating as a group.

Maersk Line and Maersk Logistics are each further divided into 17 geographical areas. The overall strategy for the business is developed at corporate headquarters in Copenhagen, with feedback from both regional and country levels. Strategic planning occurs at the regional level and execution at the country level. Each area operates according to a functional structure with such functions as line and operations, logistics, integrated sales, service delivery, human resources, finance, information systems and other container business. In other words, Maersk Line and Maersk Logistics have a global geographical organisation with functional structures. APM Terminals, however, operates with its own headquarters and its own board in The Hague, Netherlands. The headquarters of APM Terminals was placed in The Hague both to signal APM Terminals' status as an independent business unit separate from Maersk Line and to locate the headquarters closer to key European ports.

Next, we present the organisation, activities and strategies for each of these three pillars of A.P. Moller - Maersk's container business.

Maersk Line

Maersk's first liner service was established in 1928. Today, Maersk Line's network covers the entire globe with strategic centres (also called hubs) located at key points to concentrate activities on the main lines of the Europe-Far East, Transatlantic and Transpacific trade routes.

Source: A.P. Moller - Maersk

Organisation

Maersk Line purchased its first container vessel in 1973 and is now a leading world-class ocean carrier employing more than 35,000 employees in 325 offices located in more than 125 countries around the globe. The firm's status as the market-leading container liner is the result of both organic growth and major acquisitions within liner shipping, such as the liner activities of EacBen (1993), Safmarine (1999), Sealand (1999), Torm (2002) and P&O Nedlloyd (2005). In particular, Maersk Line's fleet is superior to those of its nearest competitors in terms of both capacity and projected service life (ISL, June 2006:6).

Safmarine is operated as a separate container line focusing on the Africa trade, but is expanding into other routes. Safmarine is run according to a different product profile than Maersk Line, offering services to smaller customers that are more personalised and flexible.

Activities

Maersk Line's core competence is ocean container transport. By providing inland haulage (multimodal transport services) Maersk Line is also able to offer integrated transport services to their customers. Feeder vessels, trucks, and trains allow Maersk Line to offer door-to-door transportation service on a global scale.

Maersk Line's services include:

- Containers and vessels: Modern, state-of-the-art fleet and containers in various sizes, including reefer containers for the transport of perishable foods
- Inland haulage: Multiple modes of transport
- E-commerce services: E-commerce solutions allowing for efficient exchange of data
- Customs house brokerage: Handling of customs procedures
- Refrigerated services: Services related to reefer transport
- Dangerous cargo: Transport of dangerous cargo.[7]

[7] www.maersk.com

Competitive Position and Strategy

Below we examine Maersk Line's competitive strategies and market position.

Maersk's Share of the Global Container Fleet

The container shipping industry is characterised by increasing concentration, with A.P. Moller - Maersk leading the way. Operators are increasingly consolidating through mergers and acquisitions or the formation of alliances. As of April 2006, 15 operators controlled approximately 71% of all fully cellular container ships above 1,000 Twenty-foot Equivalent Unit (TEU), equal to 80% of the global TEU capacity (ISL, 2006:6; UNCTAD, 2006:63).

Maersk Line is by far the largest operator in terms of fleet capacity. Maersk Line operates a fleet with a capacity of 1.46M TEU, equal to 18.8% of the total world fleet capacity by 2006.[8] With the purchase of P&O Nedlloyd in 2005, A.P. Moller - Maersk increased TEU capacity by 14.5% (ISL, 2006:6)

TEU-capacity of Top Ranking Containership Operators (Apr 2006)

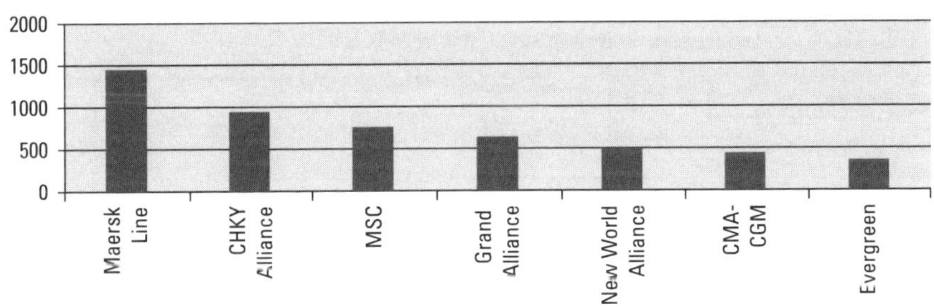

Source: ISL 2006;6

The three biggest independent carriers are Maersk Line, MSC and CMA-CGM. Eight of the top 15 operators are involved in global alliances. Twenty-five percent of the total container capacity is controlled by three alliances: CHKY Alliance, Grand Alliance and New World Alliance. By total TEU-capacity, the three largest independent carriers together with the three largest alliances control 60% of the market. These global players concentrate their activities on the Europe-Far East, Transatlantic and Transpacific trades.

---

[8] According to statistics by AXS – Alphaliner, Maersk Line's share of the total world fleet (including existing fleet and orderbook) has fallen from 18.2% by 1st of January 2006 to 16.3% by 12th of April 2007 (www.axsmarine.com/public/top100.index.php).

The Major Players in the Container Trade, 2006				
	Total		Percent Chartered	
Operator	No.	1000 TEU	1000 TEU	Av ship in TEU
Maersk-Line	431	1,460.5	53.2	3,389
MSC	229	774.4	36.7	3,382
CMA-CGM	157	468.6	62.2	2,985
Hapaq-Lloyd	127	424.8	43.7	3,345
Evergreen	123	415.4	24.8	3,377
Hanjin	80	329.2	77.2	4,114
Cosco	89	318.1	33.3	3,574
CSCL	70	312.3	49.4	4,461
NYK	99	292.9	49.3	2,959
APL	72	287.7	58.0	3,996
MOL	76	253.3	57.9	3,333
OOCL	54	238.3	37.0	4,412
K-Line	69	231.3	51.3	3,352
Yang-Ming	68	191.8	35.5	2,821
Hamburg-Sud	73	165.1	59.9	2,262
Others/unknown	757	1,595	54.0	2,107
Total	**2,574**	**7,758**	**49.6**	**3,014**
Maersk Line incl. Safmarine and P&O NL, APL incl. NOL, CMA-CGM incl. ANL-CL and Ybarra, Evergreen incl. Hatsu Marine and Lloyd Triesstino, Hanjin incl. Senator, NYK incl. TSK				

Source: ISL, June 2006:6

The Global Players: Tonnage Employed by Major Container Trade Markets, 2006			
	Europe-Far East	Transatlantic	Transpacific
Alliance/Operator	1000 TEU	1000 TEU	1000 TEU
Maersk	438.4	183.4	324.9
MSC	229.0	85.1	130.1
CMA-CGM	207.5	14.9	84.1
Evergreen	140.5	50.6	228.6
CHKY Alliance	424.3	18.6	475.8
Grand Alliance	251.3	109.3	330.9
Grand/CP Ships	–	45.6	–
New World Alliance	176.6	52.3	308.5
Total	**1,867.7**	**559.8**	**1,882.8**

Source: ISL, June 2006:7

In the Europe-Far East and Transatlantic trades, Maersk controls the highest container tonnage capacity. For the Transpacific trade, Maersk is exceeded by CHKY Alliance and Grand Alliance. In the Transatlantic trade only three global players have significant market shares, with Maersk leading (21.6%) followed by Grand Alliance (18.2%) and MSC (10.1%) (ISL, 2006:6-7).

Maersk Line's Global Market Position

Maersk Line is by far the largest single player in the industry, employing a capacity equal to 18.8% of the total world fleet (ISL, 2006:6). Despite recent consolidation, the industry remains fragmented and being the largest operator does not necessarily confer a status of market leader in general. In particular, Maersk Line's market position varies according to trade corridor and country.

The Consolidation of the Container Industry

"I think we will see further consolidation of the liner industry. Maersk Line has been involved in a number of acquisitions over time...[and] other carries are also consolidating. That trend will continue to the benefit of our customers, logistics companies will also consolidate. ... That is also taking place. This trend will continue, simply in order to service our increasingly large customers. Customers will drive the need for consolidation."

Interview with manager, Maersk South East Asia Area, Singapore, August 2006

Market Segmentation Strategy

Maersk Line's global customer portfolio includes more than 100,000 customers of which the majority are retailers (e.g.: Wal-Mart, Gap, Nike, Target, etc.). In general, customers include retailers, industrial conglomerates, and producers of consumer goods, electronics, food and beverages, healthcare products and pharmaceuticals. Maersk Line's customer portfolio is divided into three segments:

- Global key clients
- Area key clients
- Direct sales clients.

Global key clients and area key clients typically represent large MNCs seeking services on a global scale. Global key clients are companies such as Nestle, Wal-Mart, Nike, Target, and Ikea, among many others. Globally, Maersk has approximately 400 global key clients that are each supported by a dedicated global sales structure. Area key clients are clients with a regional origin and presence. The direct sales segment represents both global and local clients. Usually, the direct sales clients are clients shipping lower-value added commodities or clients that ship in corridors where Maersk Line does not have a key strategic position. Global key clients and area key clients are prioritised over direct sales clients.

Securing the accounts of large MNCs is of strategic importance to Maersk Line. These customers represent the main source of income required to recoup the high fixed costs of operating in the shipping industry and to reduce the impact of market fluctuations in the highly turbulent shipping market. Global key clients usually enter into longer-term contracts and are more likely to require additional value-added services on a global scale. Typically, they ship massive volumes of higher value-added commodities and conduct more business via E-commerce. Hence, global (and to some extent area) key clients contribute substantially to efficiency gains and economies of scale for Maersk Line.

Maersk Logistics

Mercantile, the forerunner for Maersk Logistics, was established in 1977 as a natural outgrowth of the ocean freight business. The use of containers required specialised loading (consolidation of cargo) in order to better utilize

Source: Majbritt Greve

the container space. Maersk Logistics was established in 2000 by merging the logistics expertise of Mercantile with that of the acquired company Sealand.[9]

Organisation

Through organic growth and several acquisitions, Maersk Logistics has grown into one of the world's leading providers of integrated logistics solutions. Maersk Logistics' activities span the globe with more than 200 offices in 90 countries.[10]

Activities

With the invention of containers, the requirement for related logistics services has grown. Maersk Logistics has traditionally been a consolidator, but as a natural part of its growth has also moved into information management, documentation, local transportation, customs clearance and coordination between the different players in customers' supply chains. Maersk Logistics still primarily functions as a consolidator, but while consolidation previously meant merging 'less than container loads' (LCL cargo) to save ocean freight costs, the focus today is on ensuring supply chain visibility and management by offering advanced information systems and providing value added services.

Today, Maersk Logistics' services include:[11]

- Forwarding (one point of service for handling multiple modes of transport):
  - Ocean freight
  - Airfreight
  - Landside

- Solutions (managing and improving customers' supply chains):
  - Import & export logistics
  - Warehousing & distribution
  - Supply chain development
  - Information management
  - Operational excellence (monitoring performance).

---

[9] www.maersk.com
[10] www.maersk.com
[11] www.maersk.com

The services of Maersk Logistics can be divided into transactional and solution-based services as highlighted below.

Transactional Services			Solution-based Services	
International Transport Management		Warehousing & Distribution	Import/Export Logistics	Value Added Services
Forwarding & groupage NVOCC Multi-Carrier mgt. Capacity mgt. Multi carrier contracts	Warehousing Distribution Trucking Sourcing & inventory mgt.	Consolidation Deconsolidation Information mgt. Spective Transloading Cross-docking Capacity mgt. Supply chain development	Standard consolidation Express Charter Multi-carrier mgt. Track/trace Info mgt.	Drayage Insurance Documentation Customs house brokerage

Source: A.P. Moller - Maersk presentation, Vietnam, July 2006

Transactional services are standard service solutions that do not necessarily require greater inter-organisational integration with clients. Examples include forwarding ocean freight and standard e-commerce and information tools, among many other offerings. Solution-based services are more sophisticated and complex and are typically individually tailored to client needs. Examples of such services include supply chain optimisation, advanced information technology services, advanced distribution services and dedicated facility services. Maersk Logistics is increasingly moving in the direction of more solution-based services.

Competitive Position and Strategy

Next, we examine Maersk Logistics' market position and its strategic importance for the company in the highly competitive container business.

Market Position

Maersk's diversification into providing integrated logistics services is perpetuated by the low profit-margins characteristic of the container liner business, a market reality that forces most carriers to seek new ways of increasing profits. In particular, the market for logistics has become increasingly attractive as more manufacturers choose to outsource logistics activities (Skjøtt-Larsen, 1999; Schary and Skjøtt-Larsen, 2001:230). However, today there is a tendency to define logistics very broadly, from the purchase of raw materials to the delivery of finished products. As a result, according to Maersk the market potential for logistics services is often vastly overestimated with different estimates deviating sometimes by more than 1000%. In addition, the broad scope of the market increasingly requires logistics operators to carefully position themselves in the market.

Maersk as a Cargo Consolidator

"Anyone can name themselves logistics operators. The range for logistics is very wide. That is why it is very important to define your market. Maersk's core business is consolidation branching into freight forwarding and airfreight. Traditionally we are recognised as a consolidator. Eighty per cent of our business is consolidation. This will be less in the future as we are trying to develop our other business areas."

Interview with manager, Maersk South East Asia, Singapore, August 2006

A.P. Moller - Maersk is one of the few firms that offer both ocean transport and so-called fourth party logistics services (4PL). Maersk Logistics originated as an asset-based provider operating their own vehicles and warehouses. Today, Maersk Logistics is organising supply chain management services on behalf of their clients.[12] Supply chain management services and information management tools give Maersk Logistics a competitive edge and allow Maersk to compete with more consultancy-based companies like IBM.

The market for logistics is still a fragmented market, but it is undergoing growing consolidation. The market consists of a number of players that have entered from different industry niches; ocean carriers and parcel, forwarding and warehousing companies are all expanding into providing end-to-end solutions. Information technology and management consulting companies are also expanding into supply chain management services and players such as UPS, Deutsche Post and Kuhne & Nagel are increasingly acquiring other companies in order to provide integrated logistics solutions to customers requiring one-stop-shopping solutions (Schary and Skjøtt-Larsen, 2001:228).

Maersk Logistics is one of the larger global logistics operators, competing with players such as APL Logistics, NYK Logistics, Expeditors, Kuhne & Nagel, DHL Logistics, and Panalpina. Overall, their relative market position

[12] Containerisation International, May 2001

and share is difficult to determine since they offer a wide range of different services.

The Strategic Importance of Maersk Logistics to the Container Business

Maersk Logistics operates as an independent business unit. In its function as forwarder or non-vessel operating common carrier (NVOCC), Maersk Logistics interacts with Maersk Line on market terms and also pursues 'stand-alone opportunities'. Thus, Maersk Logistics purchases ocean freight from Maersk Line or a competing carrier depending on the client's preference. Global clients typically specify a number of carriers to enhance their bargaining position and ensure capacity on a global scale. In general, however, the majority of the ocean freight is purchased from Maersk Line. Besides pursuing stand-alone opportunities, one of the strategic objectives of Maersk Logistics is to complement the business of Maersk Line. Maersk Logistics offers a wide range of products and value added services that enable Maersk Line and Maersk Logistics, through joint sales channels, to offer integrated line and logistics products. Maersk is thereby able to both meet increasing customer demand for one-stop-shopping solutions (one entry point for the purchase of freight and logistics services) and enhance customer loyalty. Whereas Maersk Line operates according to globally standardized procedures, Maersk Logistics offers clients flexibility that complements the more standardised liner business via individually integrated logistics solutions.

Customer Segmentation Strategy

As with Maersk Line, Maersk Logistics' clients mainly include MNCs within[13]

- retail (specifically footwear, apparel, sportswear, home improvement, furniture, wholesale and department stores)
- electronics (specifically hi-tech, consumer electronics and household appliances)
- fast moving consumer goods (specifically food, beer, wine & spirits, consumer healthcare products, and cold chain)
- chemicals (specifically petrochemicals).

---

[13] www.maersk.com

A large number of Maersk Logistics' customers are also key clients of Maersk Line – typically those customers that require more complex, detailed and integrated solutions.

APM Terminals

The first Maersk Line container terminal facility opened in 1975 in New Jersey, USA, as a response to the scarce port capacity of the 1970s when containerisation was just beginning. APM Terminals was established in 2001 with the acquisition of Sealand, which significantly expanded the portfolio of container terminals.

Organisation

APM Terminals is the 'third pillar' in A.P. Moller - Maersk's container business. With its own corporate headquarters established in The Hague, Netherlands in 2004, APM Terminals operates as an independent business unit within the A.P. Moller - Maersk Group with its own independent board of directors.

The Fourth Largest Terminal Operator in the World

Based in The Hague, Netherlands, APM Terminals is an independent, global container terminal owner and operator of more than 45 terminals worldwide. In 2005, APM Terminals handled a throughput of more than 24.1 million TEU's and served around 60 shipping lines. APM Terminals ranges as the fourth largest container terminal operator in the world.

Source: www.apmt.com.

APM Terminals has grown rapidly as a result of both organic growth and acquisitions. Today APM Terminals has a net turnover of 2 billion dollars and employs 18.000 people. It is present around the world (refer to map of APM Terminals port portfolio) with interests in 45 terminals located in 25 countries across five continents. Another 11 terminal expansion projects and 12 new port projects are under development, qualifying APM Terminals as one of the fastest growing container terminal operators in the world.[14]

[14] In 2006, APM Terminals achieved 18% throughput growth over 2005 (Annual Report for 2006 for A.P. Møller – Mærsk A/S, www.maersk.com).

Source: A.P. Moller - Maersk

Activities

The core activities of APM Terminals include:

- Operation and management of container terminals
- Additional services
  - Stevedoring
  - Free trade zone development
  - Acting as a port authority
  - Various other value-added services[15]

Competitive Position and Strategy

Next, we examine APM Terminals' market position and competitive strategy.

Market Position

Established in 2001, APM Terminals is a young company. Nevertheless, today APM Terminals is the fourth largest container port operator in the world, with an annual total throughput of 24.1M TEU.[16] With respect to throughput, APM Terminals is only surpassed by Hutchinson Port Holdings (51.8M TEU), PSA International (41.2M TEU) and DP World (including

[15] APM Terminals' corporate presentation, www.apmterminals.com

[16] According to A.P. Møller – Mærsk A/S' annual report for 2006, APM Terminals now has an annual throughput of 28.4M TEU (www.maersk.com).

the acquisition of P&O Ports, 36M TEU).[17] According to estimates by the Danish company Equities, APM Terminals' planned investment will make the firm the world's largest container port operator within 5 to 6 years. APM Terminals' global container port investment plan amounts to more than 15 billion dollars, more than that of any other port operator in the world (Lambek & Busch, 2006).

APM Terminals' Investment Programme

"...we do not comment on market rumours, but APM Terminals' strategy involves a significant investment programme to keep pace with global growth in the container trade, to create new capacity and to alleviate bottlenecks in support of Maersk Line's and other customers' growth."

Interview with manager, APM Terminals International B.V., Singapore, September 2006

Source: Majbritt Greve

[17] www.apmterminals.com; www.hph.com; www.dpworld.com; www.internationalpsa.com

APM Terminals' investment strategy is based on the future potential for container port development. The container transport industry is experiencing a global scarcity of port terminal capacity. Currently, container traffic is growing twice as fast as global container port capacity. In particular, the biggest constraint on container shipping today is the lack of port capacity (Lambek & Busch, 2006). According to Equities, 80% of the total global container port capacity is utilised today, and within only four years the number will reach 90%. Therefore, operators around the globe are investing large sums in new port development projects. However, again according to Equities, the number of ports under development will not be able to accommodate the global growth in container traffic (Lambek & Busch, 2006). The problem is not investors' willingness to undertake the cost of heavy port investments, but rather the scarcity of quay capacity around the world together with many governments' reluctance to allow foreign investment in this sector. Specifically, it appears that some governments are afraid of becoming too dependent on foreign investors in relation to port capacity and control.

On the other hand, China is an example of an economy that is opening up its transport sector to foreign operators and investors. Particularly within container port development, China has invited operators to invest in port development. This has allowed China sustained direct access to international markets. On a global scale, 14 of the 20 largest ports today are located in Asia, with Singapore and Hong Kong hosting the world's largest container ports (ISL, 2005:11-12).

The Strategic Importance of APM Terminals to the Container Business

APM Terminals' ambitious entry into container terminal management is being perpetuated by the increasing demand for container port capacity worldwide, a phenomenon that has made container port investments a highly profitable business. APM Terminals' global expansion means that APM Terminals today services 60 of the world's leading container lines, Maersk Line included.[18] While APM Terminals operates as a separate business unit and pursues stand-alone opportunities, there are some obvious group advantages of maintaining container port operations in-house. Operating terminals creates group advantages in the form of:

- limited exposure to port operators with monopolistic tendencies

[18] www.apmterminals.com

- improved operational planning
- dedicated hub terminals
- support for the overall strategic expansion of the route network.

While APM Terminals is an independent business unit, there are potential positive synergies associated with being part of the A.P. Moller - Maersk Group as indicated above. In controlling the ports, the A.P. Moller - Maersk Group is able to drive down costs and ensure full utilisation of a vessels' time in port. With the use of ever-larger vessels, operators need to ensure that there is adequate space and equipment to handle the vessels in port and thereby guarantee access in order to reduce the vessels' turnaround time. Slow port turnaround time is particularly costly for operators of the new giant vessels of 10,000 – 15,000 TEU (Lambek & Busch, 2006). Moreover, A.P. Moller - Maersk is able to obtain business synergies, as APM Terminals can support the strategic expansion of the route network while Maersk Line can support APM Terminals in securing volume throughput. In particular, guaranteed throughput is essential during the initial phase of operating cost intensive container terminals.

A.P. Moller - Maersk's Container Business in South East Asia

Before we turn to an analysis of A.P. Moller - Maersk's role in integrating developing countries into global value chains, we will present A.P. Moller - Maersk's organisation, activities and strategies in South East Asia. As already mentioned, Maersk Line and Maersk Logistics are organised according to area structures, one area of which is South East Asia. In the following, we focus specifically on the organisation, activities and strategies of Maersk Line, Maersk Logistics and APM Terminals in South East Asia.

Organisation and Activities

South East Asia is one of Maersk Line's largest regions as measured by volume and growth. In general, South East Asia is the world's third fastest growing region measured in terms of GDP growth, exceeded only by China and South Asia. The region hosts four of the world's largest ports with 13% of global container traffic moving through them collectively (ISL,2005:11-12). A.P. Moller - Maersk's container business in South East Asia has its headquarters in Singapore and Maersk Line is present in most South East Asian countries (refer to map illustrating Maersk's own offices and APM Terminals' main ports in South East Asia).[19] For Maersk Line in South East Asia, Thailand, Indonesia and Vietnam have the largest market potential and Thailand is currently the largest market. In accordance with the corporate structure of A.P. Moller - Maersk's container business, the South East Asia region operates according to a functional structure, with line and operating functions centralised in Singapore. Since the first arrival of a Maersk vessel in South East Asia – in Saigon in 1923 – Maersk's container business has grown significantly. Thus, for example, Maersk today hosts 41 offices[20] and employs more than 2.000 staff throughout South East Asia.

Maersk Offices (Owned)

APMT Terminals

Source: A.P. Moller - Maersk

[19] Singapore, Malaysia, Indonesia, Thailand, the Philippines, Cambodia, Vietnam, Myanmar, Brunei, and Laos.

[20] Including both wholly owned and third party agent offices.

A.P. Moller - Maersk's container business in South East Asia is represented by the following business units:

- Maersk Line
- Maersk Logistics
- Safmarine
- APM Terminals
- MCC Transport[21]
- Other container business related activities[22]

The Market Position and Strategy of Maersk Line in South East Asia

The market share of Maersk Line in South East Asia varies according to trade corridor and country. Maersk Line in South East Asia is strong in the Transpacific trade (to the US), the European trade and the Middle East and African trade, particularly that with West Africa. However, Maersk Line is not strong in the inter-Asia trade as this market is very fragmented, includes several discount operators and is subject to very low margins. On an global level, Maersk Line accounts for more than 23% of the total tonnage employed in the Europe-Far East container trade and more than 17% of the total tonnage employed in the Transpacific (between US and Asia) container trade. This places Maersk Line with the highest container tonnage capacity for the Europe-Far East trade and the third highest container tonnage capacity for the Transpacific trade (ISL, 2006:7).

The Customer Segmentation Strategy of Maersk Line and Maersk Logistics in South East Asia

The customer portfolio in South East Asia reflects Maersk Line and Maersk Logistics' global customer segmentation strategy, adjusted for the fact that South East Asia is an export intensive region.

---

[21] Feeder operator specialising in Intra-Asia services and operating 20 vessels serving Maersk Line and other carriers.

[22] A.P. Moller - Maersk presentation, Singapore, August 2006

Maersk's Customer Segments in South East Asia

"For South East Asia we focus on ten [customer] segments. These obviously reflect what is exported from South East Asia. Clearly, segments such as textiles and electronics are huge. Maersk Logistics and Maersk Line are very big within retail. We have more than 100,000 customers globally of which the majority are retailers. ... Also, we are relatively big within fast moving consumer goods ... [and] we are very strong within reefer containers. In reefer containers we are market leading both in terms of advanced technological capabilities and global market share..."

Interview with manager, Maersk South East Asia Area, Singapore, August 2006

The global trade imbalance in the shipping business is also reflected in Maersk Line and Maersk Logistics' portfolio of export and import clients in South East Asia. Maersk Line's export business accounts for approximately 80% of total volume and imports for 20% of total volume. The trade imbalance is a common problem in the container industry and mainly of a technical nature: Most countries in Asia import bulk cargo (such as iron, oil and other raw materials), but export containerised cargo (such as textiles, foods, electronics and other consumer goods). In general, shipping companies and hence customers are paying the price for returning a significant number of empty containers from the US and Europe to exporting countries.

Maersk Logistics' Customers in South East Asia

"[For South East Asia] export logistics is the prime area for logistics services. Here we aim at focusing on customers that are important to Maersk Line to create stickiness and value around the overall relationship we have with the customer. For that aim, Maersk Logistics is a critically important business unit..."

Interview with manager, Maersk South East Asia Area, Singapore, August 2006

Some shipping companies are eager to fill the space on their return vessels and may accept unprofitable cargo such as waste paper for recycling or bales of hay. According to shipping statistics, the price for shipping a 20-foot container from China to the US is on average 1,400 USD, but only 400-500 USD from the US to China (ISL, 2006:6). This price differential exemplifies the general imbalance faced by major exporting countries in Asia.

Customer Segments in Vietnam

Maersk's main export items out of Vietnam include:

- furniture, footwear and garments mainly towards Europe and the Pacific.

Maersk's imports into Vietnam are more fragmented, mainly consisting of:

- foodstuff, motor vehicles, machinery, timber and metal scrap mainly from Asia, Europe or the Pacific, but also partially from West Africa.

Interview with manager, Maersk Vietnam, September 2006

At first glance, it may come as a surprise that the import of container goods only accounts for approximately 20% of the total volume in developing countries characterised by a negative trade balance, such as Vietnam. However, many developing countries import bulk items that are not containerised and in turn export container goods. Maersk Logistics' customers are therefore also mainly export clients with respect to South East Asia. Moreover, most shipping is carried out on FOB[23] terms, meaning that the shipments are controlled by overseas buyers and retailers.

Summary

A.P. Moller - Maersk has, as a natural outgrowth of the container freight business, diversified into other container shipping related activities such that A.P. Moller - Maersk's global container business today can be seen to be organised around three key strategic units or pillars, namely Maersk Line (and Safmarine), Maersk Logistics and APM Terminals. These activities are further supported by other container related activities. With a global market share of approximately 15-20%, Maersk Line is today the world's largest container liner, by far out-distancing its nearest competitors. Moreover, Maersk Logistics and APM Terminals are among the five leading firms in their markets. Hence, there is little doubt that A.P. Moller - Maersk's global container business plays a key role in organising container traffic globally.

[23] Free On Board: This is an Incoterm indicating that sellers must load the goods on board the ship designated by the buyer and that title and risk are typically transferred at the ship's rail.

A.P. Moller - Maersk's container business includes not only transactional multimodal container transport solutions, but also highly integrated logistics solutions that cover their clients' entire supply chains. Hence, A.P. Moller - Maersk's container business plays a complex network role in many global firms' supply chains. The ability to provide global, one-stop-shopping solutions allows Maersk Line and Maersk Logistics to target large MNCs within retailing and manufacturing of consumer goods and electronics. The business of Maersk Line and Maersk Logistics is organised geographically in 17 regions. South East Asia is one of the largest regions in terms of volume and growth, with Thailand, Indonesia and Vietnam exhibiting the main growth potential. The customer portfolio in South East Asia includes global and regional retailers and producers of consumer goods and electronics, among others, all mainly focused on exports from South East Asia. A.P. Moller - Maersk's other container business unit, APM Terminals, is also well established in South East Asia. APM Terminals operates as an individual business unit but also strategically supports the other container businesses of the A.P. Moller - Maersk Group.

CHAPTER 3

The Role of A.P. Moller - Maersk in Integrating Developing Countries into Global Value Chains

Today, firms are increasingly offshoring parts of their production either to subsidiaries or to external outsourcing and alliance partners. In terms of value chain configuration, it is evident that firms' value chains are becoming not only longer and more geographically dispersed, but also more fragmented as firms devise increasingly advanced functional divisions of labour internally (Porter, 1985; Hansen et al., 2006). These developments offer enormous opportunities for developing countries. As Northern firms increasingly source activities in developing countries to reduce costs and access resources, growing numbers of developing countries (and firms in these countries) become integrated into global value chains as exporters of commodities (such as natural resources, food and beverages or textiles), or as exporters of more differentiated products (such as electronics or machinery).

The point of departure of the following analysis is that shipping and logistics' firms, such as A.P. Moller - Maersk, potentially play an essential role in providing the prerequisites for developing countries to gain access to global value chains. More specifically, shipping and logistics firms may assist in the integration of developing countries in two ways: 1) by providing physical transport infrastructure, which allows developing countries to more efficiently export and import, and 2) by reducing the transaction costs of integrating and coordinating globalised production processes, which facilitates the integration of developing country firms into global value chains.

While these potential roles of shipping and logistic firms are obviously closely related, they provide a useful analytical distinction to structure the following analysis of A.P. Moller - Maersk's container business. Consequently, we will analyze the role of A.P. Moller - Maersk's container business first with respect to building physical transport infrastructure and second in terms of integrating and coordinating globalised production processes.

With respect to building infrastructure, we will examine three interrelated services or capabilities:

- Transporting goods from port to port
- Bringing goods in-land
- Building and managing container ports

With respect to integrating and coordinating globalised production processes, we will examine four distinct potential impacts:

- Managing supply chains more efficiently
- Opening new markets
- Binding firms together in networks
- Enhancing capabilities of local firms

Building Physical Transport Infrastructure in Developing Countries

In the following, we present A.P. Moller - Maersk's role in building physical transport infrastructure. We do so by first introducing the literature on transport infrastructure and then looking at A.P. Moller - Maersk's role in: 1) transporting goods from port to port, 2) bringing goods in-land and 3) building and managing container ports.

Transport Infrastructure in the Literature

In recent years, significant technological advances within transport and communication technologies, such as containerisation and satellite communication, have resulted in a significant drop in the cost of transportation, and hence an increase in the ability to trade goods over ever larger geographical distances (Janelle and Beuthe, 1997). However, the unit cost of transportation has not diminished uniformly for all geographical destinations. Several developing countries still rely on labour intensive, scarce and poorly maintained means of transportation with consequently higher unit costs and restricted market access. According to UNCTAD, freight costs as a share of the total value of imports amount to 8% on average (but even 20-40% in some cases) for developing countries, compared to only 4% for developed countries (Pedersen, 2001:86). Hence, some developing countries still face challenges in terms of developing transportation infrastructure that can meet the requirements of the global economy. Developing countries often do not have the means to undertake cost and knowledge intensive transport infrastructure investments on their own.

Insufficient development of transport infrastructure is particularly problematic for developing countries because the quality of transport infrastructure plays an important role in explaining the location of economic activities. Firms often make investments near logistics hubs to ensure fast and reliable transport to end consumers (The Economist, 2006; Pedersen, 2001; Krugman, 1997; Dicken, 1998). Transport economists even claim that a country's stage of development is to a considerable degree a function of the capacity and sophistication of the available port facilities (Goetz & Rodrigue, 1999; Hilling, 1996; Hayuth, 1982; Hoyle & Knowles, 1998).

A.P. Moller - Maersk's Role in Building Physical Transport Infrastructure in Developing Countries

A.P. Moller - Maersk undertakes large-scale investments in designing and building state-of-the-art container transport infrastructure globally. In 2005 alone, A.P. Moller - Maersk invested 5.7 billion USD[24] in global container shipping, including container ships, containers, container terminals, and organisational expansion.[25]

Operating a global container transport network requires significant investments not only in hard technologies such as container ships and container terminals, but also in advanced information technologies and global organisational networks. With a strong financial balance sheet, A.P. Moller - Maersk can play an important role in promoting capital-intensive container shipping technologies in developing countries.

The Financial Advantages of Being a Diversified Company

"As a corporate company, A.P. Moller - Maersk has a solid financial background. With the size of our container business, our profitable oil activities, the supermarkets etc, we are highly solvent. Our diversification and size allow us to make investments and self-finance a number of initiatives that benefit our customers, us, and the society at large."

Interview with manager, Maersk South East Asia Area, Singapore, August 2006

---

[24] A.P. Moller - Maersk invested 2.4 billion USD in the purchase of P & O Nedlloyd and 3.3 billion USD in container ships, containers and container terminals.

[25] Annual Report for 2005 for A.P. Møller – Mærsk A/S (www.maersk.com)

Global Container Shipping: Transporting Goods From Port to Port

A.P. Moller - Maersk invests significantly in container vessels and containers. Maersk Line operates the world's largest fleet,[26] and in 2006 alone A.P. Moller - Maersk received 17 new container vessels, and 80,000 containers.[27] Maersk Line also operates the youngest and most technologically advanced fleet with expertise in the innovation of ship size, container technology and environmental and safety measures. Today, Maersk Line also deploys the world's largest vessels[28] (ISL, 2006:6).[29]

This significant investment in the innovation of technologically advanced vessels and containers allows for faster and cheaper transport (increased economies-of-scale and productivity), as well as the ability to trade more sophisticated goods, such as perishable items. These advantages can potentially benefit developing country firms, among others.

A Global Container Shipping Route Network

With its large fleet, Maersk Line is one of the few carriers able to operate a global route network and provide efficient round-the-world (RTW) services.[30] The RTW concept means that major trans-oceanic trade routes are linked in a complete globe-encircling network going in either an east or west-bound direction. The container flow is concentrated at major regional ports (so-called hubs) that are strategically located in the centre of major trades (e.g., Singapore). Immediate locations (so-called spokes such as Vietnam) or smaller trades feed cargo to hubs for transhipment onto the major transoceanic trade lanes.

The RTW service allows developing countries cheaper and faster connectivity to global markets. Firstly, the RTW service limits the number of port calls and allows for economies-of-scale as the service adds only marginal higher cost to the high fixed-cost required to conduct container shipping. Shippers can benefit from the unit cost advantage of interconnecting routes and having a single entry-point for the purchase of global shipping services.

---

26 Maersk Line operates 18.8% of the world's total fleet capacity (ISL,2006:6).

27 Annual Report for 2006 for A.P. Møller – Mærsk A/S (www.maersk.com)

28 Maersk Line operates a series of new container ships of more than 11,000 TEU built at the Lindoe shipyard.

29 www.maersk.com

30 Establishing RTW services is complex and requires a large fleet, a global organisation, and sophisticated IT systems to ensure global coordination.

Secondly, smaller trades, such as developing country markets, are linked by smaller feeder vessels allowing for more frequent shipments and hence faster access to global markets. As developing country firms often compete in industries where price and time to market are some of the key competitive criteria, cheaper and faster access to markets may be of critical importance.

The case of a large furniture manufacturer in central Vietnam exemplifies the importance of feeder connectivity (see box). This manufacturer of low cost furniture faced high transport costs in comparison to its competitors in China and Indonesia mainly because the products had to be trucked from central Vietnam to HCMC. By inserting feeder ships from central Vietnam to HCMC (where the products could be transhipped to Singapore and then onwards to the final destination), MCC Transport (a feeder subsidiary of A.P. Moller - Maersk in South East Asia) was able to reduce the costs of transport and hence increase the competitiveness of the manufacturer.

Opening Opportunities for Trade in Furniture

"Our buyer [a global furniture retailer] is the driver behind both Maersk and my factory. Only the buyer has the ability to compete worldwide and set-up businesses in small alternative countries. ... Together with Maersk, they are the reason we can operate a large business here employing 7.000 people and creating growth for the town and the town port. These companies can do business in areas that are non-standard."

Manager of a foreign owned furniture manufacturer in central Vietnam, HCMC, 2003

Bringing Container Shipping to Developing Countries

While other firms may avoid entering developing countries due to the difficulties of operating in countries with significant state bureaucracies or the lack of basic infrastructure, Maersk Line enters even 'difficult' locations, such as those in Africa or parts of Asia (Jønssons, 2006:3). With its global presence, Maersk Line enables even smaller trades to be connected to global markets via its services.

Connecting Developing Countries

"For South East Asia, which is eleven countries..., some of these countries have the status of being developing countries. We as A.P. Moller-Maersk, have the organizational and financial strength to set up organizations in all these countries that will allow us to pursue business opportunities, develop infrastructure...And we have within the company over the years build a lot of competences in operating in what other people would call more difficult locations..., we are both global and local. When we operate locally, we do it under the terms and conditions that apply, but with the global strength of A.P. Moller-Maersk...operating in developing countries is often more motivating, because the difference you make to society is much greater, much more significant, and more measurable than in developed countries. Connecting Saigon or Daressalam makes much more difference to these locations than operating in Rotterdam, Los Angeles..."

Interview with manager, Maersk South East Asia Area, Singapore, August 2006

A.P. Moller - Maersk's promotion of container shipping technologies on a global scale may be crucial to developing countries. Containerisation allows for mechanical handling of cargo, thus reducing transit time, labour costs, pilferage and damage. It also makes transport more effective, reducing the turnaround time of ships in port[31] (Hayuth, 1982; Gilman, 1977). The containerisation of developing countries' trade traffic may have a strong impact on the opportunities and competitiveness of developing country producers since the ability to consolidate cargo in containers allows producers to ship smaller volumes on a more frequent basis, trade more sophisticated goods and ship much more cheaply than previously possible.

[31] Seaborne cargo was previously carried in break bulk. Cargo was loaded and discharged in small lots and individual items were man handled in the port and onboard the ship. Containerisation implies a mechanisation and thereby reduction of costs and transit time. It makes transport more effective, reducing the turnaround time of how long ships need to be in port (Hayuth, 1982:13; Gilman, 1977:11).

Maersk as an Early Mover in Vietnam

Maersk was among the first foreign container shipping firms to enter the Vietnamese market. With the purchase of the East Asiatic Company's container liner traffic, Maersk gained access to the Vietnamese market. It quickly developed the container traffic in Vietnam from two Inter-Asia lines to global container liner services. Previously, the Vietnamese shipping sector relied on general cargo and bulk technologies and lacked connection to an international container transport network. Today, Maersk has a rather unique position in Vietnam: It is the first carrier to have been granted the license to operate as a 100% foreign owned operator. It is also the largest operator, ensuring abundant container shipping capacity for the rapidly growing Vietnamese economy.

Global Multimodal Transport: Bringing Goods In-land

A.P. Moller - Maersk's container business invests in other modes of transport or subcontracts with multimodal transport operators for rail, trucking and airfreight, and invests in logistics asset-based activities (such as warehouses, distributions points, inland depots, container freight stations, etc.) to ensure inter-modal connectivity and reliable door-to-door transport for their clients. Investments in in-land transportation such as rail and trucking are mainly undertaken by local independent companies within the A.P. Moller - Maersk Group, whereas asset-based logistics activities mainly are undertaken by Maersk Logistics.[32]

Source: A.P. Moller - Maersk

[32] Maersk Line is a non-asset owning entity, and hence does not invest in facilities.

Investments in in-land transport and asset-based logistics activities are small compared to the sums A.P. Moller - Maersk invests in container terminals, container vessels and containers. Investments in in-land transport and asset-based logistics activities are mainly undertaken when these will support the global key clients with whom Maersk Line maintains longer term and more integrated relationships. Often such in-land facilities are dedicated to specific clients, as is the case in Vietnam where Maersk Logistics has invested in dedicated warehouse facilities for major clients within the footwear industry. Moreover, investing in in-land transport and logistics activities in developing countries is often not feasible due to the lower cost structure of local operators. In general, the extent to which A.P. Moller - Maersk invests in in-land transport and asset-based logistics activities varies from country to country: In Vietnam, Maersk Logistics has invested in fully-owned warehousing operations and subcontracted with local and international trucking, rail, airfreight and warehouse operators. In Thailand, A.P Moller - Maersk has invested in a fully-owned trucking subsidiary that operates as an independent unit. In Africa, A.P. Moller - Maersk has historically played a larger role in in-land infrastructure development, probably due to a lack of local transport service operators, combined with the fact that several countries on the African continent are land-locked.

Global Port Infrastructure: Building and Managing Container Terminals

APM Terminals undertakes large-scale investments in state-of-the-art container terminals. Container terminals are the most critical investments in the industry. There is a great deal of pressure globally to build and expand container terminal capacity to meet the global growth rate of containerised cargo.

Promoting Container Port Development Globally

"As an industry player, we are pointing wherever we operate to the needs of having efficient infrastructure to achieve a more efficient economy and ability to compete. Honestly, we do not need to state it, it is as banal as 2 and 2 is 4....But some regimes do not have the ability or the luxury to have such vision or see that far, either because they are only there for a short time and have other objectives, such as sitting in a leadership position, or simply because the funding is not there locally or internationally."

Interview with manager, Maersk South East Asia Area, Singapore, August 2006

Pressure on Global Port Capacity

"...the biggest problem in our industry is infrastructure capacity! With the growth rate of the industry in general, port terminals cannot follow suit. Some places worse than others."

Authors own translation, interview with manager, Maersk South East Asia Area, Singapore, August 2006.

In the following, we will examine the case of APM Terminals in South East Asia in more detail to exemplify APM Terminals' role in building container port facilities. APM Terminals in South East Asia partly owns and manages two ports, the port of Tanjung Pelepas in Southern Malaysia (in the Malacca strait) and Laem Chabang port in Thailand. An additional port, Cai Mep, is under development in Southern Vietnam. In the following, we will focus on the port of Tanjung Pelepas (PTP) and the port of Cai Mep.

The Port of Tanjung Pelepas

The port of Tanjung Pelepas is Maersk's regional hub in South East Asia. APM Terminals plays a significant role in the development of Tanjung Pelepas as APM Terminals holds a 30% investment share and has full management control of the terminal operation. The port is situated in Southern Malaysia in the confluence of the world's busiest shipping lanes. As detailed below, the port of Tanjung Pelepas potentially facilitates accessibility to and from developing countries in South East Asia in several ways.

Source: Majbritt Greve

First of all, the port of Tanjung Pelepas has the capacity to cater to the impressive economic growth rates of containerised cargo in the region. Tanjung Pelepas is a young port, first opened in 2000, with an annual throughput of 4.2M TEU and with potential capacity to meet future economic growth in the region. The world's largest port, Singapore, with throughput of 22M TEU annually, is on the other hand unable to meet future growth due to restricted space options. Consequently, Tanjung Pelepas is today the fastest growing port in the region (ISL, 2005:10-11).

Facts About the Port of Tanjung Pelepas

- A 70/30 joint venture between MMC (Malaysian Mining Corporation) and APM Terminals respectively.
- APM Terminals manages and operates the port.
- Throughput in 2005 was 4.2M TEU
- Maersk Line and Evergreen are the main liners and 60% of the throughput is accounted for by Maersk.
- 95% transhipment hub, 5% import/export to/from Malaysia
- Nominated as the most productive port in the region (34.62 gross moves per hour).
- Includes an industrial & commercial free zone

Source: Presentation by Port of Tanjung Pelepas, Malaysia, August 2006

Secondly, in acting as a transhipment hub with advanced, efficient equipment, PTP provides fast and reliable access to global markets for countries in the region.

Thirdly, Tanjung Pelepas offers benefits to container shipping operators by providing a competitive alternative to the port of Singapore, which previous had a relatively monopolistic position in the region. Due to its unique location, the port of Singapore has historically been the epicentre of international trade and the only transhipment hub in the region. The arrival of port of Tanjung Pelepas has potentially stimulated competition on price and quality levels of transhipment port services in South East Asia. Competition on price and economies-of-scale advantages may trickle down to shippers in the region and contribute to cheaper container transport.

Fast and Cheap Access to Markets

"The transport industry has undergone dramatic change over recent decades...so that transportation cost per unit today is negligible. This trend has been driven by increasing containerisation, increases in vessel size, and development of large container terminal facilities equipped with new, modern, and fast equipment and information systems, which can facilitate turnover of huge volumes in a short time. In other words, our business is driven by economies of scale ..., which benefits exporters in producing countries to bring their goods to the market, and enable consumers fast and cheap access to consumer goods. A few ports including Tanjung Pelepas are transhipment ports acting like hubs, where big shipping lines can optimize their route networks by feeding to/from smaller ports and interchanging volumes between vessels."

Interview with manager, APM Terminals, Singapore, September 2006

Fourthly, the port and its surrounding area facilitate hinterland growth through the creation of logistics and industrial clusters in the region of Southern Malaysia (as well as parts of Indonesia and Singapore). The Malaysian government has identified the Johor region as the core economic development area in Malaysia, and the PTP and its surrounding area have been designated and developed as a logistics and manufacturing industrial centre.[33] The centralisation of infrastructure and physical facilities in the region provides firms with advantages in terms of locating manufacturing, storage, consolidation and procurement activities. Hence, this integrated logistics and manufacturing centre has attracted more than 100 companies, up from less than 10 in 2000 when the port was opened.[34] The commercial free zone has attracted major logistics operators such as Maersk Logistics, Schenker Logistics and BMW, and the industrial free zone has attracted companies such as Flextronics, Kimberly-Clarke and JB Cocoa[35].[36]

[33] 400 acres are designated as a free commercial zone reserved for distribution, logistics and warehousing activities. 600 acres are marked as a free industrial zone for hosting light, medium and heavy manufacturing industries.
[34] Presentation by Port of Tanjung Pelepas, Malaysia, August 2006
[35] A Malaysia-US joint venture cocoa processing plant
[36] www.ptp.com and presentation by Port of Tanjung Pelepas, Malaysia, August 2006

Creating Hinterland Economic Growth

"APM Terminals has the most significant impact on infrastructure development [within the A.P. Moller - Maersk Group]. The investment in a port is one thing, but a port must also be connected to the rest of the world. So, typically, the investment brings about a highway or the construction of a railroad. Then you choose to build an industrial park nearby and suddenly it evolves into an industrial area with access to cheaper transport. … However, I must add that most often we alone do not decide where and when to build a container terminal … [rather] governments will typically issue a tender."

Interview with manager, Maersk South East Asia Area, Singapore, August 2006

The Cai Mep Terminal

In Vietnam, containerised cargo volumes are growing by approximately 19% annually and represent the fastest growing and most critical segment for seaport development. Insufficient infrastructure to support the high growth of container exports and imports is a growing problem. Estimates show that despite the governments' plan for future infrastructure development, the current network will not be able to support the growth of the Vietnamese economy. Vietnam's recent accession into the WTO is expected to put further pressure on Vietnam's infrastructure network. Consequently, major manufacturers, such as Nike, are starting to voice their concern. Nike's exports out of Vietnam represent more than 3% of Vietnam's total exports and more than 9% of its manufactured exports.[37] If current estimates prove correct, Vietnam's infrastructure will be under significant pressure in a few years time, forcing manufacturers and retailers sourcing in Vietnam to consider switching sourcing strategies.

Providing Container Port Capacity to Vietnam

"In my view we have an incredible value in what we do for a country like Vietnam, for development in Vietnam. If Maersk were to withdraw from Vietnam, it would be a big loss for the country. It would mean that larger firms would consider relocating…It would remove large capacity from the market."

Interview with manager, Maersk Vietnam, July 2006

[37] Vietnam Business Forum, Mid-Term Meeting, Hanoi, June 2006

In order to provide for the rapidly expanding economy and meet the needs of Nike and other firms operating and sourcing in Vietnam, APM Terminals, in partnership with Saigon Port (under the Vietnamese transport ministry), is building Vietnam's first deep-sea facility, Cai Mep.

Securing Mass Volume Sourcing from Vietnam

"Take Nike – an important part of their decision to source from Vietnam depends on the government's decision to build deep-sea terminal facilities. ... Through APM Terminals we have the financial background and the competences to partner with the Vietnamese government in developing a deep-sea facility. ... It ties in with our vision to create global opportunities for customers in Vietnam."

Interview with manager, Maersk South East Asia Area, Singapore, August 2006

Cai Mep will be situated near Saigon with adequate depth to service larger vessels and is expected to be completed by 2009. Indirectly, the Cai Mep terminal will enhance the competitiveness of the Vietnamese economy and enhance Vietnam's competitiveness with respect to countries like China, which today hosts several advanced deep-sea ports, some of which are among the fastest growing terminals in the world in terms of tonnage (ISL, 2005:11-12). The Cai Mep terminal will also allow Vietnam to become a transhipment point for other neighbouring countries.

How Cai Mep May Enhance the Competitiveness of the Vietnamese Economy

- Enabling direct access to international markets
- Enhancing capacity and reducing congestion
- Enabling cheaper freight to/from Vietnam by:
  - Reducing transhipment points
  - Allowing use of larger vessels
  - Reducing deviation time and lead time
  - Employing advanced technologies to increase productivity

Summary of interview with manager, APM Terminals B.V., Vietnam, July 2006

Integrating and Coordinating Globalised Production Processes

In the following, we will present how A.P. Moller - Maersk plays a role in connecting developing countries to buyers and sellers across the globe by acting as an intermediary that coordinates and integrates firms' value chains across geographical distance. Our focus will be on Maersk Logistics and to a lesser extent Maersk Line. We start out by introducing the logistics literature on inter-firm supply chain collaboration and then move on to analyze A.P. Moller - Maersk's role according to four dimensions:

- Managing supply chains more efficiently
- Opening new markets
- Bringing firms together
- Enhancing the capacities of local firms

The Logistics Literature on Inter-firm Relations

As firms increasingly outsource parts of their production and internal functions to external partners, their supply chains become longer and more intertwined. Hence, the involved parties in the supply chain become more

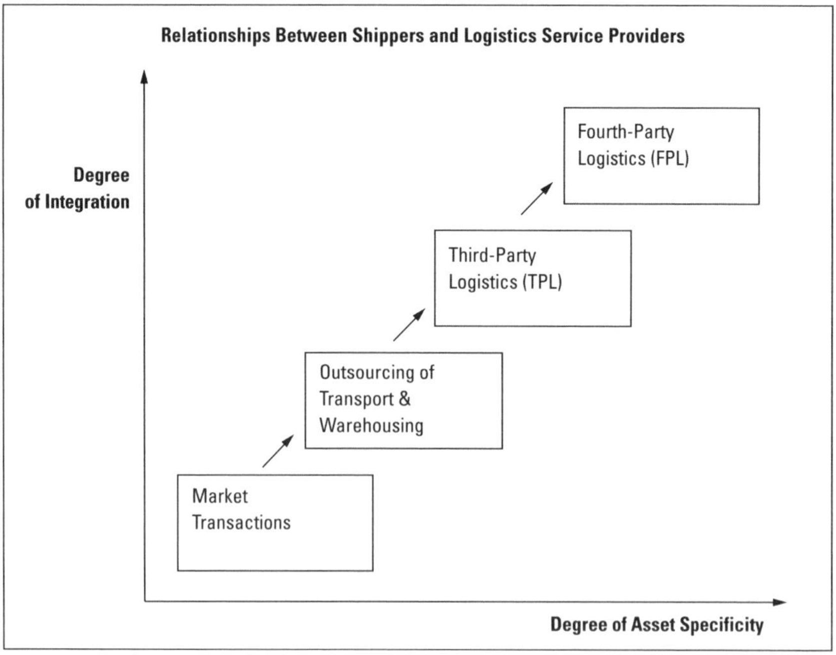

Source: Schary and Skjøtt-Larsen, 2001:228

interdependent on each other's resources and competencies and supply chains become increasingly complex and difficult to manage (Skjøtt-Larsen, 1999; Berglund et al., 1999). To give an example, the world's largest retailer, Wal-Mart, deals with more than 60,000 suppliers in their network in the US alone (The Economist, 2006). According to Bagchi and Skjøtt-Larsen, managing supply chains today requires exceedingly close coordination and integration of processes among firms in the chain:

> *The links are often several echelons deep on both (the) procurement and distribution side(s). ...These links are nowadays enabled by inter-organisational process integration involving close coordination among partners providing access to each others business and manufacturing plans* (Bagchi and Skjøtt-Larsen, 2003).

In this situation, logistics providers come to play an important role, not only as providers of geographical and transactional connections between firms, but also increasingly as integrators and coordinators of entire global supply chains. The more integrated logistics services the shipper requires, the larger a role logistics providers come to play. Thus, moving from the purchase of a simple arms-length market transaction, such as ocean freight, to providing a complete package of logistics services requires an enormous leap in the scope and depth of cooperation. The changing relationship between shippers and logistics service providers is illustrated and explained in the figure above. More specifically, the relationship can be divided into four stages have the following characteristics:

1. Market transactions involve no specific assets or integration between the parties. They represent arms-length relations that rely on short-term contracts and involve mainly a single activity, e.g. transport. Price is the main competitive criteria.

2. In outsourcing of transport and warehousing, the shipper outsources logistics activities (physical operation), but maintains management control internally. This stage involves a limited degree of asset specificity and integration. Standard solutions are implemented and the main competitive criteria is price.

Source: Majbritt Greve

3. In third party logistics, there is greater commitment by both parties involving integration of operations (e.g.: interfacing information systems and inter-organisational teams) and longer-term binding agreements. Co-operation is based on mutual trust and open information sharing. The 3PL provider may invest in dedicated facilities and other tangible and intangible assets (e.g.: personnel training, equipment, warehouse operations, etc.). Services are tailored to the individual client.

4. The stage of fourth party logistics refers to the highest degree of cooperation between shipper and logistics operator and involves a greater scope of services of more strategic importance to the shipper. It involves a greater degree of outsourcing by the shipper of management and logistics services, ranging from traditional services such as warehousing, transportation and value added services to managing and optimising the supply chain with a focus on information technology and global coverage. A lead logistics provider (one point of entry) is often responsible for securing the provision of the whole package of logistics services. The large 3PL providers are moving in this direction. Relationships are based on long-term contracts or even joint ventures involving system integration and inter-organisational teams at various management levels. Asset specificity is high and entails investments in, among other things, dedicated facilities, specialised equipment and human assets (Schary and Skjøtt-Larsen, 2001).

Creating Value for Clients

- Operational efficiency (better performance/cost ratio)
- Economies of scale via the integration of operations (e.g., in warehouse operation)
- Vertical and horizontal integration of providers (sharing resources and focusing on core competences)
- Supply chain management and integration (optimising customers' service levels and improving customers' supply chains through conceptual logistics skills)

Source: Berglund et al., 1999:63

A.P. Moller - Maersk's Role in Integrating and Coordinating Globalised Production Processes

Maersk Logistics is both an asset-based provider operating their own vehicles and warehouses, as well as a non-asset based provider undertaking supply chain management services on behalf of their clients. Hence, Maersk Logistics is able to offer the whole package of logistics services required for meeting the needs of MNCs. In providing a broad range of logistics services, Maersk has come to play a key role in coordinating and integrating firms' supply chains, and hence in potentially linking firms in developing countries to global value chains. Other third party logistics providers in South East Asia are for example DHL, UPS and Schenker, which could possibly have the same effects.

Maersk Logistics' Technology and Information Management Tools

- Spective: leading edge supply chain visibility solution
- Startrack airfreight
- Advanced back-end systems
- Vendor connectivity solutions
- E-booking and documentation (M*Power Shipper)
- Electronic Data Interchange (EDI)
- Barcoding
- Radio frequency identification (RFID) competencies

Source: www.maersk-logistics.com

Managing Supply Chains More Efficiently

Maersk Logistics' service package includes a wide range of services, from simple arms-length and standardised transaction based services to more complex and tailor made solution-based services involving significant organisational integration with clients. Common to all these services is that the client outsources logistics in order to reduce costs and/or improve service quality. Thus, Maersk Logistics may create value for their clients through the optimisation of supply chains. By managing clients' supply chains, Maersk Logistics both enables clients to manufacture and source efficiently on a global basis and enables firms in developing countries to be linked to global customers.

Creating Value Chain Transparency

"One of our critical needs in our business is visibility. We need to be able to see the cargo before it arrives at destination and control the delivery time. ... The critical logistics need of all global players is accuracy and time [accuracy of information and timing]. Maersk has the financial background to invest in information systems globally."

Interview with the Lead Logistics Manager of a global textile retailer, Singapore, August 2006

An example of how Maersk Logistics facilitates the more efficient management of supply chains is their provision of supply chain transparency: In acting as an intermediary, Maersk Logistics plays an important role in creating supply chain transparency across geographical distance and across different actors in the chain. For instance, Maersk Logistics has technology and information management tools that create global supply chain transparency for shippers.[38] Bridging the information gap is particularly vital in a developing country context with low market transparency and poor information technology capacity. Maersk Logistics offers a wide range of e-commerce and information transparency technology services that can be adapted to countries with limited information technology capacity (refer to the box above).

[38] Investments in IT systems make up a significant part of A.P. Moller - Maersk's total investments (Annual Report for 2005 for A.P. Møller – Mærsk A/S, www.maersk.com).

By receiving a reliable flow of information, Maersk Logistics' clients can level out fluctuations in the supply chain and prevent distortions. The more information these clients are able to obtain on the partners in their supply chains, the better they are able to plan, coordinate and streamline production and inventory (e.g.: in the form of lean manufacturing and just-in-time production).

Creating Value Chain Transparency in Vietnam

"Our system is interfaced with our clients systems, so each time they have an order from a factory in Vietnam, we get the order details in our system. Purchase order number, stock keeping unit, number of cartons and so on. ... The shippers are pulling all this information out of our system and re-using it for the booking process. ... It makes the process easier for the shippers and minimize mistakes during manual typing. M*Power is web-based, so there is no need for complicated interfaces. We have a project team which are facilitating workshops for the shippers and are teaching them how to use the systems."

Interview with manager, Maersk Vietnam Ltd., Vietnam 2006

The global key clients interviewed for this study all stated transparency as one of their most critical needs for operating across developing countries in South East Asia. A large global food manufacturer, for example, markets products with a short shelf life requiring a short transport lead-time. As retailers within 'Fast Moving Consumer Goods' are consolidating, food manufacturers are increasingly forced to take on activities related to controlling inventory and product shelves in the retailers' stores. Hence, supply chain transparency becomes increasingly critical.

Opening New Markets

Maersk Logistics may assist customers in sourcing goods anywhere in the world, reaching new markets more quickly, and supporting entry in new markets. Through their global presence, Maersk acquires and develops a knowledge of local markets that is shared with clients. With an integrated sales organisation, Maersk Line and Maersk Logistics, as an added service, provide their local knowledge and market intelligence to a range of customers, thereby potentially reducing the customers' transaction costs of entering or operating in foreign markets.

The transaction costs of gaining reliable and professional market information and of searching for and dealing with partners is often significantly higher in developing country markets than in more developed markets.

Entering New Markets

"We are often among the first container shipping companies to enter new markets, which means that we are able to build up a profound knowledge of local markets. It is my impression that customers respect our local knowledge and wish to learn from us. ... When we present our markets to customers, customers request information on the political and economic stability of the country. How secure is the country politically, economically, terrorism wise and so on."

Interview with manager, Maersk South East Asia Area, Singapore, August 2006

The market intelligence that Maersk makes available to their clients can include anything from a general presentation of the market and A.P. Moller - Maersk's business, including for example country statistics and economic facts, to more in-depth market information on the business climate, business segments and the coordination of contacts in the respective market. The specificity of the information partly depends on the client relationship – the more integrated the relationship the more market specific knowledge will be provided as an added service.

Maersk Logistics' Global Services

"We need a key global service provider that can support us wherever we go. ... Maersk has the financial background to invest globally ... and the willingness to grow with us. ... Maersk and APL are the strongest providers. Other carriers do not have the logistic dimension or only on a small scale. Maersk and APL are globally oriented."

Logistics Manager for South East Asia of a global manufacturer and retailer of textiles and garments, Singapore, August 2006

Providing Market Intelligence

"Those of our customers where we have an intimate close relationship and partnership approach, we will of course share with them our intelligence that we have access to in terms of projects, bottlenecks and constraints. If they visit any country, the Maersk office will always be there to assist, getting around and meeting the right people etc. in that sense we are supporting our customers... it is courtesy to our customers, part of the package. It is a differentiator, because there is no doubt that with Maersk's presence in basically all locations and with own people and with experiences developed over the years what we can offer is worth a lot to our customers and I think they appreciate it as well."

Interview with Manager, Maersk South East Asia Area, Singapore, August 2006

In cases where Maersk Logistics operates as a 3PL or 4PL, the relationship with the client is frequently based on mutual trust and open information exchange, and hence particularly close cooperation takes place. Maersk Logistics has client management teams at both origin and destination that study the needs of clients. As part of the sales strategy, they may update and advise clients on market developments and market opportunities. Obviously, this information exchange takes place according to strict client confidentiality.

Providing Market Intelligence in Vietnam

"Overseas buyers often visit us with a big sales force... and ask questions about infrastructure, politics, investments, what are the pitfalls and so on. They want to see the port, the container freight station and warehouse. We show them around and inform them of the business environment in Vietnam and we bring them into contact with vendors, with factories..."

Interview with manager, Maersk Vietnam Ltd., July 2006

Bringing Firms Together

Facilitating trade relations is traditionally considered the task of embassies, trade departments or trading companies. However, with Maersk's local market intelligence, Maersk may be able to help clients identify reliable and professional suppliers in the local context.

Introducing Clients to New Suppliers

"Typically, for some clients, Maersk Logistics will assist them with identifying new vendors, trying to secure new capacities for sourcing if they want to increase out of Vietnam or move from lets say China, Thailand, or Indonesia. It is part of the ILM [Integrated logistics management] group's responsibility to all the customers in the initial phase to allow them to secure new supply lines."

Interview with manager, Maersk Vietnam Ltd., July 2006

Thus, in key client partnerships where it operates as a 3PL or 4PL, Maersk Logistics may assist in securing new supply lines by introducing key clients to local manufacturers in import and export markets. Maersk's dedicated client sales and service teams may cooperate with their clients to identify new suppliers that can meet the clients' compliance mandates. By facilitating the gathering of information about potential local partners, Maersk can reduce the cost of finding and dealing with new suppliers, a process that may prove particularly challenging and costly in developing countries. Moreover, by facilitating the creation of direct links between clients and local manufacturing firms (as opposed to links through agents or trading companies), Maersk may help clients bypass costs in the chain and obtain lower unit costs. In linking clients to local firms, Maersk Logistics also facilitates access to global value chains for local firms. Access to international markets is one of the main challenges for developing country firms, which for the most part find it difficult to mobilise the resources and skills to market themselves abroad. It should be noted, however, that the extent to which Maersk's market information and sourcing services play a role in attracting global clients to developing countries varies across countries and sectors (see box above). Moreover, these services are reserved for a limited number of clients, in particular large global key clients.

Maersk's Strategic Importance to Clients' Sourcing Strategies

"The question is if the global retailer, not operating in Vietnam, would in any way be affected by Maersk's involvement in Vietnam. The answer to that in my books would be: no. I don't think Maersk stand alone would be able to change their position, to change their sourcing from e.g. Thailand to Vietnam. I don't think company X [a global retailer of sportswear] would be guided. But if company X had done their homework and wanted support to source from Vietnam, then we would be able to play a role. Allow them to come here and see the factories and explain the dynamics behind how the infrastructure and how the future looks from our perspective. I don't think they stand alone would take a decision purely based on what we or any other transport company have to say...but if they were to get all that information that we provide on their own, they would have to be here 1 to 2 years to get a sense of the business environment. We as an international company can speak the same language, their language, and explain some of the challenges we foresee in the future and some of the positive developments."

Interview with manager, Maersk Vietnam Ltd., July 2006

Enhancing the Capabilities of Local Firms

The extent to which developing country firms become linked to global value chains obviously depends on the local industry's ability to meet the compliance mandates of global retailers. For example, one of the challenges in the Vietnamese manufacturing industry is the scarcity of large vendors that have the size, quality and professional skills to meet the requirements of global MNCs. Large MNCs are looking for vendors that can deliver mass volumes of medium to high quality products at low costs, and at the same time adhere to public and private standards related to working conditions, the environment, and health and safety. Moreover, MNCs are looking for suppliers with a professional 'mind-set', that is suppliers that understand the importance of delivering products on time, a competitive requirement crucial to global retailers operating with lean supply chains. As a consequence, Maersk Logistics in Vietnam mainly cooperates with foreign owned suppliers (approximately 70% of the suppliers are foreign owned and 30% locally owned).

To enhance the capabilities of local firms, in some instances Maersk Logistics guides and trains local firms in meeting the standard operating procedures of key clients.

Vendor Management

As argued above, enhancing the capabilities of local suppliers may arise as a direct effect of Maersk Logistics' vendor management services or as an indirect effect of Maersk Logistics' strategy to open the local market. In the following, we will elaborate upon the direct effect of vendor management services.

Source: Majbritt Greve

Maersk Logistics offers vendor management as part of their supply chain management services to ensure that vendors meet the compliance mandates of Maersk Logistics' clients. Vendor management means that once a contract between the buyer and supplier has been signed, Maersk Logistics will, if required by the client, provide guidance to the vendor on how to work with the client and, in some instances, train the vendor in the client's standard operating procedures. Furthermore, Maersk Logistics can monitor the performance of the vendor to ensure operational efficiency (e.g., in meeting shipping deadlines). Vendor management allows clients to limit their organisational presence in the country, as well as save on the resources needed for the training and control of vendors. Monitoring vendor performance may be a particularly valuable service in a developing country context where the costs of controlling contracts, so-called policing and enforcement costs, may be relatively high due to market and institutional failures.

Adding Value for Local Vendors

"We [Maersk Logistics] do add value to the vendor, but at the end of the day, we are both serving our final client...But the vendors are also our customers and we see them as potential clients. We try to help them whenever they have issues".

Interview with manager, Maersk Vietnam Ltd., Vietnam, July 2006

From a developing country firm perspective, vendor management can be viewed as one way of lowering entry barriers and enhancing the capabilities of local firms. Moreover, the pressure to comply with production and shipment deadlines may spur greater efficiency in the vendor's own supply chains. However, some vendors interviewed for this study perceived Maersk Logistics as less flexible than other service providers and as mainly representing their client's interests. For example, Maersk Logistics may levy a penalty on the vendor if cargo is delayed for shipment, this as part of the firms' so-called exception management.

Summary and Discussion

In this chapter, we have analysed the role of A.P. Moller - Maersk's container business in building container transport infrastructure and integrating and coordinating globalised production processes. We have seen that A.P. Moller - Maersk's container business potentially facilitates the integration of developing countries and their firms into the global economy. This occurs partly through the provision of global connectivity as a result of building ports and transport route networks, and partly through a reduction in the transaction costs of cross-border inter-firm collaboration within supply chains. Thus, we find that the activities of A.P. Moller - Maersk's container business may pave the way for both foreign firms to enter developing country markets and developing country firms to access to global markets.

However, these findings should be interpreted with some caution. Firstly, assessments of the effects of foreign direct investments face the issue of 'counterfactuals', in other words we cannot predict which effects would have occurred had the investment not taken place (Lall, 2000). In the context of this study, we may see that A.P. Moller - Maersk's investments within container shipping have facilitated the integration of the Vietnamese economy into the global economy, however we are unable to predict what would have happened had A.P. Moller - Maersk not invested. For instance, we cannot know if other local or global container shipping firms would have moved into the same market, applying similar strategies and yielding similar effects.

Client Follower or Instigator?

"Maersk to a large extent, follows the interests of their key clients. We place investments so that they follow the business of the client. But if we look at the large investments, typically ports, they are placed strategically based on the short and long term estimates of the development of the market. I.e. here we almost dictate where demand should occur. Clients' sourcing strategy to some extent depend on the location of ports, in contrast to shipping, which is very demand driven. Here we can insert capacity, vessels, according to where the demand is. The strategic location of ports, however, is more supply driven, customers have to pay attention to where future ports will be placed. The location of the port depends on the larger macro economic trends ... [and] we calculate with a 50 year time frame."

Interview with manager, Maersk Vietnam Ltd. Vietnam, July 2006

A second note of caution is related to the issue of establishing causalities in assessing the effects of foreign direct investments. Often, it is difficult to determine whether the foreign direct investment is a cause or consequence. In the context of this study, for instance, it can be debated whether A.P. Moller - Maersk's investments paved the way for foreign MNCs to enter Vietnam or rather the investments of foreign MNCs paved the way for A.P. Moller - Maersk. On the one hand, it can be argued that A.P. Moller - Maersk mainly follows large international importers and retailers into developing countries. These clients are becoming ever larger and with their growing bargaining power they can increasingly dictate the changes and developments within container transport. On the other hand, while some of A.P. Moller - Maersk's container business investments, such as adding vessel capacity to a destination or investing in warehouse facilities, may indeed be dictated by important clients, other investments may not directly be influenced by current client requirements. For instance, it is evident that APM Terminals' investments in port facilities are largely based on longer-term estimates of macro-economic trends rather than on specific demands from major clients. With the growing global pressure on port terminal capacity and the growing focus of global manufacturers and retailers on streamlining supply chains, proactive investments by port operators such as APM Terminals may play an increasingly important motivational role in MNCs' locational decisions.

On balance, we would argue that the discussion of whether investments by A.P. Moller - Maersk's container business are cause or consequence of global value chain integration is a rather philosophical one. Instead, we believe that it is more fruitful to see the integration of an economy into global value chains as a process that takes place in close symbiosis between governments, large MNCs and transport firms, and that especially the role of the latter has been largely overlooked in the literature until now. Hopefully this study has uncovered some of the potential aspects of the role that container shipping may play in opening a developing economy, thus contributing to filling a lacuna in the received literature.

CHAPTER 4

Conclusion

Main Findings

In this study, we have analyzed the role of A.P. Moller - Maersk's container business in integrating developing countries and their firms into the global economy. In general, the role of transport has until now been the subject of rather shallow analysis in the academic literature and the literature has largely failed to fully understand transport as an integral and holistic part of economic development processes. Building on an extensive empirical analysis of A.P. Moller - Maersk's container business in South East Asia, we have attempted to address some of the limitations of the existing literature. Overall, we found evidence that A.P. Moller - Maersk's container business may play an important role in the integration of global production processes, not only by moving goods from A to B and coordinating multiple modes of transport, but also by coordinating and integrating increasingly atomized production processes at a global scale. More specifically, we distinguished between effects related to building physical transport infrastructure and effects related to integrating global production processes.

A.P. Moller - Maersk assists developing countries in establishing physical container transport infrastructure by building and managing ports and warehouses, and by building and managing sea and land transport connections that move goods between countries, firms and consumers. With an investment programme of more than 5 billion USD annually, a globe encircling route network of 125 countries and a position as the market leader, A.P. Moller - Maersk plays an important role in spreading advanced container transport technologies to developing countries. A.P. Moller - Maersk's container transport investments provide developing countries with cheaper and faster access to international markets, thus potentially making the developing countries more attractive to MNC producers and buyers. Moreover, A.P. Moller - Maersk's container transport investments may enable developing country firms to ship smaller volumes on a more frequent basis, trade more sophisticated goods and deliver their products to international markets at a cheaper price.

Furthermore, A.P. Moller - Maersk's container business may play an important – and possibly growing – role in integrating developing countries into global value chains by reducing the transaction and coordination costs of entering developing countries for major MNC clients. Thus, A.P. Moller - Maersk facilitates, its clients entry developing into countries by creating economies of scale, by delivering operational efficiency and by optimizing and improving supply chains. It may further allow its clients to source from a larger number of countries, over ever longer geographical distance, without necessarily having a physical presence in the specific markets. It may reduce transaction costs of market exchange by building up knowledge of the local markets, and sometimes making this knowledge available to its MNC clients. Based on its local knowledge, A.P. Moller - Maersk (and in particular Maersk Logistics) may assist key clients in identifying potential business partners. Once the client and a local firm have engaged in a contract, Maersk Logistics can offer so-called vendor management services that enhance the monitoring and control of the local vendor. Finally, such vendor management services may enhance the capabilities of local firms in meeting the compliance mandates of global firms and create efficiencies in the local firms' own systems. In sum, by managing supply chains more efficiently, by opening new markets, by bringing firms together and by enhancing the capabilities of local firms, A.P. Moller - Maersk may play an important role in connecting developing country firms with foreign MNCs, thus contributing to economic development.

Caveats and Avenues for Future Research

While this study concluded that A.P. Moller - Maersk may play an important role in global value chain integration, it also stressed there are some important qualifications to this conclusion. First, the study discussed whether the detected development effects are unique to A.P. Moller - Maersk. Thus, we do not know if other transport solutions would have produced developmental effects similar to those produced by A.P. Moller - Maersk had the company chosen not to enter the country or region in question. Second, the study discussed whether A.P. Moller - Maersk is the cause or the consequence of global value chain integration. Thus, while there is an indication that A.P. Moller - Maersk may in some instances be an instigator of global value chain integration, paving the way for large MNCs to enter emerging markets, it appears that A.P. Moller - Maersk in other instances is more of a client follower. On balance, we argue that the opening of a developing country economy takes place in a synergistic relationship between the strategies of large MNCs and the strategies of transport providers such as A.P. Moller - Maersk, within the confines of government policy and regulation.

Overall, more in depth research is needed in order to reach firmer conclusions regarding the role of container shipping investments, such as those of A.P. Moller - Maersk, in integrating the developing world into the global economy. Such research could include studies of A.P. Moller - Maersk's activities in other developing countries and regions and/or of the broader transport sectors' role in opening developing countries to world markets.

List of References

Altenburg, Tilman (2000): "Linkages and Spillovers between TNCs and SMEs in developing countries", in United Nations Conference on Trade and Development, *TNC-SME linkages for development*, p. 3-57, Geneva, UNCTAD.

Bagchi, Prabir K. and Skjøtt-Larsen (2003): "*Integration of Information Technology and Organization in a Supply Chain*", International Journal of Logistics Management, vol. 14 (no. 1), pp. 89-108.

Berglund, Magnus; Laarhoven, Peter V.; Sharman, Graham and Wandel, Sten (1999): "Third-party logistics – is there a future?", *International Journal of Logistics Management*, vol. 10 (no. 1) 1999, p. 59-70.

Blomström, Magnus and A. Kokko (2000): "Multinational corporations and spillovers" in Blomström, Magnus and Kokko, Ari and Zejan, Mario, *Foreign direct investment: Firm and host country strategies*, p. 101-133, Macmillan, Basingstoke, UK.

Containerisation International (2001): "Close encounters of the fourth kind", p. 42-47, An Informa Group Publication, UK, May 2001.

Dicken, Peter (1998): *"Global Shift – Transforming the World Economy"* (3rd edition), London, UK, Sage Publications.

Dunning, John H. (1997): *"Alliance Capitalism and Global Business"*, London, UK, Routeledge.

Fjeldstad, Oystein D. and Stabell, Charles B. (1998): Configuring Value for Competitive Advantage: On Chains, Shops, and Networks", *Strategic Management Journal*, vol. 19 (no. 5), p. 413-437.

Gereffi, Gary (1994): "Capitalism, Development and Global Commodity Chains", In Sklair, Leslie (ed.), *"Capitalism and Development"*, London, UK, Routledge.

Gereffi, Gary; Korzeniewicz, Miguel and Korzeniewicz, Roberto P. (1994): "Introduction: Global Commodity Chains", in Gereffi, Gary and Korzeniewicz, Miguel (eds.), *"Commodity Chains and Global Capitalism"*, Connecticut, US, Greenwood Press.

Gereffi Gary; Humprey, John; Kaplinsky, Raphael and Sturgeon, Timothy J. (2001): "Introduction: Globalisation, Value Chains and Development" *IDS Bulletin*, vol. 32 (no. 3), July 2001, p. 1-8.

Gilman, S. (1977): "Optimal shipping technologies for Routes to Developing Countries" in Brooks, Mary R. et al.: *"Maritime Transport"*, UK, 2002, MPG Books Ltd.

Goetz, Andrew R.and Rodrigue, Jean-Paul (1999): "Transport terminals in new perspectives", *Journal of Transport Geography*, vol. 7, 1999, p. 237-240.

Hansen, M.W.; Pedersen, T. and Petersen, B. (2006): *Danish Investment in Developing Countries-A Global Value Chain Perspective*, CPH: CBS Press.

Hayuth, Yehuda (1982): "Intermodal transportation and the hinterland concept", *Tijdschrift voor Economische en Sociale Geografie,* Vol. 73 (no. 1).

Hilling, David (1996): *"Transport and Developing Countries"*, London, UK, Routledge.

Hoyle, Brian and Knowles, Richard (1998): *Modern Transport Geography* (2nd edition), London, UK, John Wiley & Sons.

Institute of Shipping Economics and Logistics, ISL (2006): *"Shipping statistics and Market Review – Focus: Container and general cargo shipping"*, No. 6, June 2006, Germany.

Institute of Shipping Economics and Logistics, ISL (2005): *Shipping statistics and Market Review – Focus: World Port Development,* No. 11/12 November/December 2005, Germany

Janelle, Donald G. and Beuthe, Michel (1997): "Globalisation and research issues in transportation", *Journal of Transport Geography,* Vol. 5 (no. 3), p. 199-206, UK, Elsevier Science Ltd, Pergamon.

Jønssons, Signe (2006): "Afrikas stjerne er lyseblå…", *Månedsavisen Udvikling,* No. 3, April 2006, Udenrigsministeriet, Danmark.

Krugman, Paul (1997): *Development Geography and Economic Theory,* paperback edition, UK, MIT.

Lall, S. (2000): *FDI and Development: Policy and Research Issues in the Emerging Context,* QEH Working Paper Series – QEHWPS43, Oxford.

Lambek, Bjørn and Busch, Granzow, Niels-Peter (2006): *"A.P. Møller – Mærsk på vej til at blive verdens største havneoperatør"*, Politiken, 30. August, 2006.

Lauridsen, Laurids S. (2003): "The role of the state in linkage formation between TNCs and local Thai enterprises", paper presented at the workshop on *Understanding FDI-assisted Economic Development* 22-25 May 2003, TIK-centre, University of Oslo.

Leinbach, Thomas R. (1995): "Transport and Third World Development: Review, Issues, and Prescription", *Transport Research-A,* Vol. 29A (no. 5), p. 337-344.

Lieb, Robert C. (2005): "*The 3PL Industry: Where It's Been, Where It's going*", Supply Chain Management Review, vol. 9 (no. 6), p. 20-27.

Meyer, Klaus (2005): *FDI spillovers in emerging markets: A literature review and new perspectives,* DRC Working Papers no 15, London Business School, March 2003, pp. 1-52

Narula, Rajneesh & Marin, Anabel (2003): *"FDI spillovers, absorptive capacities and human capital development: evidence from Argentina"*, Second draft 19 July 2003, Merit – Infonomics research memorandum series, Maastrict, The Netherlands.

Pedersen, Poul Ove (2001): "Freight transport under globalisation and its impact on Africa", *Journal of Transport Geography*, Vol. 9, p. 85-99, UK, Pergamon Elsevier Science Ltd.

Porter, M. (1985): *"Competitive Advantage: Creating and Sustaining Superior Performance"*, Free Press, New York.

Rabach, Eileen and Kim, Eun Mee (1994): "Where Is the Chain in Commodity Chains? The Service Sector Nexus", in Gereffi, Gary and Korzeniewicz, Miguel (eds.), *Commodity Chains and Global Capitalism*, Connecticut, Greenwood Press.

Schary, Phillip B. and Skjøtt-Larsen, Tage (2001): *"Managing the Global Supply Chain"*, Copenhagen, Denmark, Copenhagen Business School Press.

Skjøtt-Larsen, Tage (1999): "Interorganisational Relations from a Supply Chain Management Point of View", *Logistics Management*, 1 Jg., Ausg 2, p. 96-108.

The Economist (2006): *"Survey: The Physical Internet"*, June 17, Vol. 379, Iss. 8482; pg.3, London,UK.

United Nations Conference on Trade and Development (2006): *"Review of Maritime Transport, 2006"*, United Nations Publications, New York and Geneva.

Internet sources

www.maersk.com
www.apmterminals.com
www.hph.com
www.internationalpsa.com
www.dpworld.com